THIS

FLOATING

WORLD

Published by
Landmark Books Pte Ltd
5001 Beach Road
#02-73/74
Singapore 199588

Landmark Books is an imprint of
Landmark Books Pte Ltd

ISBN 978-981-14-8561-9

Printed in Singapore

THIS FLOATING WORLD

この浮世

Gwee Li Sui

◦LANDM△RK◦BOOKS◦

He beggars his life.
Now he empties his mind for
a world to flower.

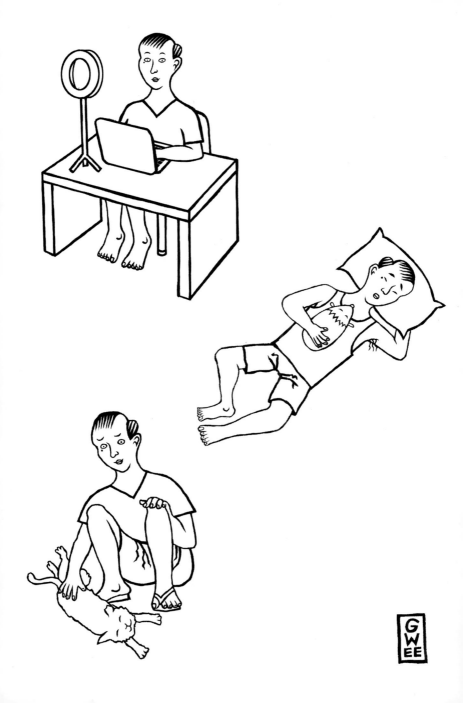

1   The crock is broken
    and words are gushing out to
    make room for a void.

2　　The cold air turns cool.
　　In the garden, a cat laps
　　up a pool of tears.

3　　O truth! I have no
　　being if I don't choose you.
　　Opinions darken.

4   I haven't stepped in
     this river before. Not this
     river. Not this I.

5   God is silent and
     my heart gapes. How it covets
     one meaningful act!

6   People with too much
time are making people with
too much time angry.

7   Who are the poor? If
we can know, then some will get
more help than others.

8   Don't think of all your
problems the Gahmen can't solve.
Focus on the world!

9   I tell my MP
I get all my exercise
collecting cardboard.

10   Adultery is
     coming! Lock up your spouse and
     disable wifi!

11   I don't drink or smoke,
     nor do I gamble. I don't
     have the money to.

12 Now that I pay less
    to see a doctor, I can
    sell more tissue packs.

13 Row, row, row sampan
    gently down the stream. A cruise
    ship is but a dream.

14 How pure the words we
    say in darkness! In the day,
    they taste of poison.

15 To save our own skin,
    we call one another out.
    Good old Chinese purge.

16   Fake news, plagiarise,
        misattribute, misquote, spread
        hate and fear – bye bye!

17   All your life you will
        sweat until you retire
        on death. Dust to dust.

18 Midnight approaches.
As I walk, I hear a voice
behind calling me.

19 An omelette is
    an omelette except to
    a politician.

20 Miss Postmodern asks
    Captain Colonial for a
    dance. A bad idea.

21   It is like a cat
        I have on my face to stroke
        any time I want.

22   Is the child of a
        god a god? She commands:"Don't
        worship my father!"

23   We are ready for
a minority PM!
But Da Man declines.

24   A songwriter turns
Nobel laureate. The times,
they are a-changing!

25   Singapore welcomes
      an infestation of big
      fat dancing rodents!

26   I have a partner
      and I have a small space. Unh!
      Flat priority.

27   Weapons and cigars
couldn't assassinate you.
But Death is a pro.

28   Parents decry a
comic. On the main display,
Fifty Shades of Grey.

29   Objectified, you
     choked the beast to death. Princess
     and my General.

30   Kings of the Terrain
     get mired in politics.
     Still stuck at a port.

31   Some folks look good. Some
look good by making others
look bad. Some look bad.

32   The mystery cat
reaches into his pouch. There
he finds my childhood.

33 She forgets to heat
    the pot and continues to
    serve me cold coffee.

34 The heavens sing! The
    city becomes a river,
    its people otters.

35   If you run and fall,
       even with an umbrella,
       you will still get wet.

36 The world awakes to
    your brand-new reality
    show: America.

37 Our young people lack
    entrepreneurial dare.
    Chiong ah! You chiong ah!

38   Your kind has always
     lived here. But Fate did not warn
     you of bad neighbours.

39   Ants never get lost.
     See how they march in line and
     sniff another's ass!

40   In a line, in the
      cold, the workers stay up for
      opening hours.

41   Kindred meeting, steam-
      boat eating, mahjong playing,
      money depleting.

42 You tired, you poor,
    you huddled masses yearning
    to breathe free – heraus!

43 The killing goes on.
    Another family flees
    to a foreign land.

44 It screams like thunder
    and falls – all three hundred years
    of dying, ending.

45 Love is dead. But not
    while the world glides on the wings
    of fallen angels.

46   Into the den of
his subduers Percival
marched, white as a flag.

47   How is it a name –
this sound made with the knuckles
of Yamashita?

48   Some call it fire
     rainbow, some iridescent
     cloud. Some say Ah Kong.

49   Are you Gwee Li Sui?
     I have been calling your name;
     why don't you respond?

50　"We need people to
　　challenge authority," say
　　people who didn't.

51　"Baa baa, yes-men, have
　　you criticisms?" "Yes sir,
　　yes sir, three brag-ful!"

52 The lonely city
   is my wilderness. Daily
   I seek a true path.

53   Committee upon
      committee. The emperor
      becomes sequestered.

54   "You have lost your heart!"
      "Yes, untie our hands so that
      we can grope for it!"

55 Skywards, the dull grey
   steps turn gold. But look down and
   they are an eyesore.

56 Tale as old as time,
   fear as old as crime: fundies
   and LGBTs.

57 My body that is
    broken for you. Eat this flesh
    and remember me.

58 The preacher's snake oil
    appears and disappears on
    Carousell. Magic!

59   A baby suckles
      on a boob on a train. More
      mouths drop wide open.

60   一粒苹果还
      是一个？我的华语
      一块一块的。

61　我在华文班
　　整天讲鸟话。现在
　　我吃马铃薯。

62　Troll the Right. Troll the
　　Left. Get jailed. Get money from
　　fans. Buy plane ticket.

63   Now out, the sun dries
      the wet pavements. But the rain
      in my heart falls on.

64   Milk is milk. You buy
      expensive milk to have smart
      kids – but are you smart?

65   An online post gets
      rebuked by a minister.
      Cat photos follow.

66   Missing wheels, missing
      saddles, missing pedals… Not
      what bike-sharing means.

67   I am eating. Why
       do you come near? Want to steal
       my lunch? I bite you!

68   "Good day, Europa!"
       "Don't forget to pay your bills
       first, Britannia."

69   A haikuist dies.
      His friends remember him in
      a pause between words.

70   Down the hall of time,
      in the chamber of our minds,
      the midnight banging.

71   I hold you close, your
      thorns to my flesh. When this is
      over, we shall feast.

72   Hello, China? Can
      give us an invitation?
      We love you long time.

73   Days ago, I could
      feel you curl under my breath.
      Little did we know.

74 Teachers are leaving?
   Students are abandoning
   the arts? So ta ta.

75 I sink into your
   many layers and taste the
   patience in your love.

76 Said the logician
    to the guru: "Never say
    never say never!"

77 All the colours in
    my words don't matter. You see
    my body's darkness.

78   Years later, some kid
      braves the cave to check if the
      tiger still has teeth.

79   Please go through again.
      In the last paragraph, last
      line, I say sorry.

80   Two great legs of stone,
nothing else. The desert wind
traces the king's name.

81   In love with his words,
she chooses a living death.
How he maims her faith.

82 My eyes stay open
    to pray. The darker domain
    keeps me in focus.

83 When they came for you,
    I did not speak out. Later,
    I wrote this haiku.

84   When siblings live in
     harmony, the very act
     honours their parents.

85   Once you fade enough
     into the forgetting night,
     there are only words.

86 Words are not a will.
A will is not a house. A
house is not a home.

87   The beanstalks light the
fire that cooks the beans. Yet
they had the same roots.

88   None to rein them in,
the hounds look out in wonder.
Each gathers a scent.

89   I go on display
   to serve him again. Some say
   I am abducted.

90   With bells, joss sticks and
   words, different prayers are formed
   mere metres apart.

91   At dusk, the long fast
ends. Forgiveness is a feast
before a new day.

92   Hello, police? Here
got some people anyhow
make police report!

93   When it was over,
     some left. Others hid to grieve.
     You did the sai kang.

94   Truth has no witness.
     Speculation has many
     mouths and many tongues.

95   Accusations swirl.
       Truth becomes a poisoned cat
       both dead and alive.

96   The ocean in the
       sky falls on a parched city.
       The people sizzle.

97   All show the same face.
      Only one doesn't wonder
      within who farted.

98   Flames from a single
      household grew, frying rows of
      innocent houses.

99   The cats fight on the
Persian rug, unravelling
a lifetime of work.

100 Just two buttons hold
my national green around
my prosperity.

101   Where is the proper
      forum to debate about
      the proper forum?

102   Small states must act like
      small states! His big idea gets
      roundly diminished.

103 Who are you in whose
    dream I am awake that I
    cannot sleep tonight?

104 The spirits among
the grass welcome us. Their stone
homes are without doors.

105 Loong, if anything
happens, look after mama,
meimei and didi.

106 Kin and foes alike
    are human. Why sue one group
    until their pants drop?

107 The new signalling
    system meant to solve delays
    is causing delays.

108 Devoutly he cleans
     and supervises himself.
     An unsung hero!

109 A beauty pageant
     draws flak. Out of its mockers,
     so much ugliness!

110 To think of me and
     to let my community
     accept me as one.

111 The girl rose to help
     make nasi padang to sell.
     O the aroma!

112 Only form holds up
     the words. The poet is no
     longer at the heart.

113 Lawyers and loan sharks
     are not the same. That said, you
     lose money to both.

114 From the dock, grey and
   haggard, they scanned for faces.
   Wet eyes greeted them.

115 The hungry dog bites
   the hand that feeds it. Now the
   hungry dog hungers.

116　All of what you write
is your words. But not all of
your friends are your friends.

117　Death bellows across
the oceans. It threatens to
scorch the skin of earth.

118 Sun in my eyes, sand
     in my shoes, distant laughter,
     childhood memories.

119 She watched his maypole
     overtake any amount
     of trigger warnings.

120   In the eye of a
      nation's celebration, a
      boy's middle finger.

121   Long after he's gone,
       the man on TV still cries.
       Yesterday once more.

122   Where the sun looks down
       with favour, there the shadows
       are also darkest.

123 How is a nation
    with more smartphones than people
    smart? Think about it.

124 O sweet thing, don't you
    know you're my everything? Yes,
    you are. Yes, you are…

125   What will you do when
        hate speaks its hate? When darkness
        meets you in the day?

126   Along Shanghai streets,
        a mountain tortoise. All its
        cash can't buy chestnuts.

127 Cashless remittance?
My folks won't have it. My folks
in the netherworld.

128 We – flickering in
neon, in a small space – make
passion possible.

129 I am here in a
     tissue pack on the table,
     an absent presence.

130 With one contender,
     it is hard to tell: did she
     win or did she lose?

131 No thanks! Think tanks that
    think they can tinker will get
    a tinkle and tank.

132 She guides the future
    with red ink. Her inflictions
    will reverberate.

133 Free from foreigners'
       power! Now, to the end, bound
       to one another.

134 What can my words do?
       They are killing you. Your homes
       are burnt on my screen.

135 With enigmatic
     eyes, you would read to us the
     day's news. Our angmo.

136 We saw the future
     and acted and it changed. But
     who sees our future?

137 Life is a shithole.
    It doesn't get better when
    I come out to breathe.

138 The mother fears for
     her growing child. His new claw
     cuts into her mind.

139 Inside, a bony-
     legged hag motions to you.
     A question is asked.

140 Fate cannot break you,
     nor nature subdue you. The
     spirit is the man.

141 The tall poppy sees
     far and cries aloud: "Come join
     me in politics!"

142 The void deck extends
       a shadow as she saunters
       into the state car.

143 Kept in a square box,
       a big cheesy circle I
       eat in triangles.

144 Through the suppression
     of urban concrete, some wet
     dream breaks. A geyser!

145 Caesar could not speak.
     At the rostra, Cato went
     on and on and on.

146 Smearing, name-calling,
    mud-slinging, news-faking, shit-
    stirring, hand-washing.

147 We never got to
    read your famous magazine.
    Really. No, really.

148 Our current neighbours
     are shy but friendly. Daily
     a stream of men comes.

149 Happy hour at
     last! The earth's drinking habit
     threatens to drown trains.

150 Together, let us
    progress in our studies. But
    take care of your health.

151 News of job losses.
    Sadness felt by people who
    don't buy newspapers.

152 The fruit basket still
    smells after we toss out the
    fruits. The problem is…

153 I apologise
    and shall be responsible.
    Those others failed us!

154 We share kueh dadar,
     pineapple tarts, murukku
     and diabetes.

155 Everyone wishes
     to heal. Yet no one reaches
     out to anyone.

156 The den reeks of filth.
     Jabba paws the new girl while
     his aides look away.

157   In a future of
      bright nights, a couple cradles
      a three-eyed baby.

158   I know sacrifice.
      I, too, give back to others
      in my cushy job.

159   She discovers home
    in her cooking. Their grouses
    cut her off again.

160   You trained your feet to
    walk on tightwire. But your
    audience wanted clowns.

161　Come, let's see who wins –
　　　your parents' Lamborghini
　　　or my wife's Nissan!

162　The thought shapes questions.
　　　The questions crunch numbers. The
　　　numbers divide us.

163 When will it all be
     over? The morning ends with
     a bang and whimpers.

164 Reliving childhood,
     it threw her out. She had to
     visit a sinseh.

165   A small group of you
       neutralising the good work
       by the rest of us!

166   In the night of age,
       your truth shone even brighter
       and taught us to see.

167 He sleeps amid the
chatter in the room. All the
world is lost to him.

168 At dawn I hear you.
All through the day I feel you.
At night I see you.

169 She holds the dolls close
     to her breast, amassing gifts
     for her grown-up kids.

170 First the sky darkens,
     then a rumbling. But the rain
     is taking its time.

171 Keep your mind pure and
you practise virtue. All else
is mere performance.

172 Saying nothing more,
     you ask me to pray. I kneel
     in my eyes' darkness.

173 Hope has found its way
     to your lips! In the streets, your
     heart dances away.

174　Some beast slams your gut.
　　　You wake to bites of lightning,
　　　red spouts from your neck —

175　Down comes the angry
　　　rod of heaven to smite you,
　　　fast as you may run!

176 The shoppers push in,
     screaming and grabbing at things.
     A reverse jailbreak.

177 Major Tom to Ground
     Control, I hear knocking from
     outside my tin can –

178　You left me alone
　　　too long. Now my balls are hard
　　　and not nice to suck.

179　Round and round we go
　　　like it matters. The water
　　　cascades through a pump.

180 The City of Peace
cuts up the world. Its ancient
stones survive in vain.

181 The void remembers
its occupants, dragging chairs
through its neighbours' sleep.

182 As the world sleeps, a
baby cries. Destiny keeps
its parents awake.

183 Floor tiles popping up
like a choir and folks dressed
up like Eskimos.

184 I am too cute! Come
     closer, little ones, so that
     I can get a snap.

185 So much happiness
     in store for people with their
     buckets of sunshine!

186　He said she said, but
　　　she didn't. He heard they heard,
　　　but nobody did.

187　The sun is barely
　　　out. Puddles of morning rain
　　　wait to be rippled.

188 The days flit away.
The cut grass has to decide
who is taller now.

189 Can oily hands take
the heat? A well-regarded
name goes up in flames.

190 I am fake news. You
are fake news. We are fake news.
That makes me real news.

191　The Instagram girl
　　　smiles coyly. Today she sounds
　　　just like my Gahmen.

192　The skies roar into
　　　me. Then comes the perfect rain,
　　　dousing my parched world.

193 The drains are drowning
    from shallow love. My feelings
    for you are unquenched.

194 Not yours but mine: the
    responsibility of
    making things happen.

195 Not among chums but
       men at loggerheads, the one
       with knuckle-dusters.

196 Putting money in
       your bank is auspicious, no
       matter when it's done.

197 "The word to use is
'peoplekind'," says the person
to the woperson.

198 A dummy in a
red sports car drifts in space for
millions of years. Why?

199 My love, hold me as
I hold your cups! Take us to
the dirty corner!

200 "Si geenas, you don't
go write letters to the courts
for your residents!"

201   With or without a
      hex key, this bed you cannot
      assemble yourself.

202   Manly I am when
      I pay for dates. Less so when
      I get criticised.

203   I am a tenured
professor. I have earned the
right to say what I

204   Did we ever think
your horseshoe luck could ward off
the love of money?

205 Nothing changes, not
the pay, the hours, the room
of helpless faces.

206　It rose with the day,
　　　the blood sun. The boots of Death
　　　trampled my city.

207　Winter is coming.
　　　The fire of discontent
　　　swells within our hearts.

208 Children still dying
   in their sanctums. All their lives
   bleeding out in lead.

209 Come, let me make you
   fishers of men. Catch me in
   my fleeing sampan!

210 He breathed fire, drawn
to the seat of power in
Heaven and on earth.

211 Floating tangerines,
the maidens whisper wishes.
Lo, men in blue come!

212 Speak up! Look at me!
What you fear is mythical –
defy your bosses!

213 Save the world, but wear
your vulnerability
outside. It calms us.

214 I release poems
       into your day. Will they be
       appreciated?

215 Folks of Hougang are
       Hougangsters. Tampines's
       are Tampenises.

216 She weathers the storm
      of their interpretations
      and will not be cowed.

217 My childhood ship of
      fools is sunk with him. O Death,
      why you so liddat?

218 Some in many books
     say less than you in one. This,
     too, is poetry.

219 As history ends,
     a star falls into itself
     and becomes darkness.

220 Irrational but
     constant, unenclosable
     within a haiku.

221 I fine-dine, speaking
     good English. You speak Singlish
     and eat cup noodles.

222 Keep still and listen.
All the words you hear turning
in your heart are mine.

223 "What is truth?" Pilate
asked aloud. But my Gahmen
wanted clarity.

224 Architects of our
future are upset to lose
a perk from the past.

225 "Chicken rendang has
     to be crispy." Two angmo
     judges got deep-fried.

226 So we disagree;
     let's talk it out. No one needs
     to get sued or jailed.

227 Why are you reading
fake news? Read our articles
behind a paywall!

228 My future lives in
the past, in how I exhume
it for the present.

229 Of course, your private
information is safe with
us. And us. And us.

230 Feet to feet he washed
before a new commandment:
"Love one another."

231 Who are you who call
     me friend and show me my heart
     in my cheating kiss?

232 Everywhere we look
     for somebody without the
     relevant skill set.

233 There he is under
     our beds yet again! This time
     funding a website!

234 Come rub me down for
     electricity. I am
     warm against the night.

235 The rain punishes
     you. But I go out untouched
     under your long arm.

236 Life is beating in
     seconds. I want to feel the
     contours of each thought.

237 A Buddha is hard
     to meet, his words hard to hear.
     This is how you bloom.

238 In winter cool and
     summer green – how you were a
     season of your own.

239 You do not age as
others do. With daybreak, your
wings are young again.

240　You called from within.
　　How could I have known before
　　that I was outside?

241　The old ghosts – they are
　　home. Who can be kept
　　free from his shadow?

242 Her soul, scattered with
     the dust of the land. It roams,
     howling for justice.

243 So many fancy
     handbags, but none big enough
     to hide a face in.

244 Schoolkids in a field.
     Do they detect the rigged game
     society plays?

245 What father whose child
     asks for bread gives him a stone
     to keep him in check?

246   Two fat men on a
pleasure island. This chance for
world peace not so slim.

247   Onlookers rejoice
while politicians swoon. A
dictator in town.

248 All this while as you
took to eat into the world,
what was eating you?

249 In the bowels of
the beast, the children weep for
their absent parents.

250 The president had
a thought. It's marvellous what
Milo did for her.

251 You misinform. They
connive. We always listen
with an open mind.

252　I lie on a side,
　　　counting my days. How I took
　　　you for a ride twice!

253　Go digital, go
　　　whole-of-nation, aim high, stay
　　　humble – change is here!

254 Today they are down,
     but yesterday they were up.
     Tomorrow who knows?

255 I touch you in your
     words. I read the curves of your
     lips and kiss your soul.

256 We want you not to
     do what we want but to want
     to do what we want.

257 However you dream,
      your boy child is mine. You can
      never win this game.

258 The question is: can
      we trust you to trust us to
      trust you to trust us?

259 Life is short. Talk it
out. Forgive. Your friends are friends.
The media isn't.

260 Outsmarted, the Smart
Nation smarts. Guard against the
treachery of words.

261   They came and went, those
thieves of night. In the morning,
we fasten our doors.

262   I hide you inside
my shadow and you blush. A
red rose in the night.

263 This haiku is free;
     it can't be any good. Why
     do I write at all?

264 They hunch around the
     carcass, etherised by a
     smell of rotten flesh.

265 The birthday boy brought
the sun. Now everyone's face
is as red as his.

266 Liquid fire leaps
to me as I fall. I am
the volcano now.

267   "Pay me peanuts and
      I will be a monkey!" A
      monkey warns others.

268   Years on, the taunting
      still roars. The head is a room
      with sleeping termites.

269 Didn't read the book.
    Haven't watched the film. But the
    trailer makes me mad.

270 A sudden rain of
    white petals on a hearse. An
    empty kopitiam.

271   Spirits lifted, the
annual custom ends. Back
to work tomorrow.

272   All my years sworn to
this cause: to mould young minds with
my mouldy old mind.

273 Flutterings. Mynahs
      on unreturned trays. Tissue
      paper in the wind.

274 Wind puffs up empty
     bladders. Only one thing I
     know: I know nothing.

275 Come away from this
     shadow within your true form
     while there is still light!

276 "Would you like to meet
with the world's oldest statesman?"
"Yes! What could go wrong?"

277 They move with torches
and pitchforks. At the far end,
a voice of kindness.

278 With age, there are games
you get better in. The young
don't understand this.

279 Why keep an anal
code in the penal code? Whose
pen is mightier?

280 Two roads diverge. If
we take the one less travelled,
the nation is doomed.

281 Game theory kicks in.
If the otters win, the croc-
odile doesn't lose.

282 Our position not
to have a position was
Ah Kong's position.

283 One minute of bliss
in a flawed democracy.
See you tomorrow!

284 Sleep a night under
     rockets. You don't have problems:
     you are the problem.

285 Listen – the sound of
     darkness! My tubs of ice cream
     dripping in the fridge.

286 If you don't drive a
     car, I can drive mine. Let's give
     brisk walking a try!

287 The moon enters whole
     into the darkness of my
     mouth. Who hears it scream?

288 Thought you understood
when you joined up. We don't take
profits — why should you?

289 I work late. I head
to the hawker centre. Why
is nothing open?

290 Mid–life, I lost all
     my wisdom. My mouth swells with
     gibberish and blood.

291 It's great at the top
until we aren't. Then the
metrics need to change.

292 Two hundred chemi-
cal reactions before the
chemistry exam.

293　The children decide:
　　　"Let us let our children and
　　　their children decide."

294　We are all riding
　　　the same escalator up.
　　　Progress without change.

295 If I was born poor
     and rose to be an elite,
     am I an elite?

296 While we were dreaming
     to be an olive, we have
     turned into a pear.

297   The night is howling.
      We wear upon our bodies
      the souls of the dead.

298   Who I am I rub
      in your faces. Feel the fat
      of my privilege!

299 This poem makes no
      reference to whom poems
      may not refer to.

300 In his age, Ah Kong
      dreamt again of paradise.
      He was not yet free.

301 I just met you. This
is crazy. My Gahmen says
we're baby-ready!

302 Bismillah! Is this
the real life? Must I be Ma-
chiavellian?

303 A nation marvels.
      In a race of white horses,
      is there a dark horse?

304 Two male hands converge
      upon a dress. That has made
      all the difference.

305 Now the Ultimate
     Nullifier is set on
     the Seeder of Worlds.

306 Every day I drink
     fresh milk and stand in the sun
     for thirty minutes.

307   It begins with the
      flicker of candlelight: the
      dying of evil.

308   Walk lightly this way
      that is widening with words.
      There are thorns in clouds.

309   We have the right to
      set rules that make us look bad!
      It's what we pay for!

310 Don't test the waters
     between us. Your only ship
     we like is friendship.

311 While the world bawled, in
     you I found rest. But you were
     leading me astray.

312 But I really can't
stay on and watch your mummy
kissing Santa Claus.

313 We never put all
our eggs into one basket.
Because Malaysia.

314   Roused and ready, a
      bird prepares to land. Will it
      hit a tall building?

315   My hands fall asleep
      between the soft sheets. My eyes
      flutter to awake.

316 Not that we can tell
how the days will get longer.
Tonight we eat moons.

317 I sing the body
electric. The chopper slips
from my hand. I fall.

318 'Twas the day after
Christmas. All over the web,
the trolls are stirring.

319 The night is young, but
neither of us is. What are
we even thinking?

320   Addiction evolves.
      The scales fall off and flesh out
      something leathery.

321   I thank you and set
      you free. You spin into the
      belly of the chute.

322 The banks are soft with
     beginnings. Today we plant
     both our feet in time.

323 Your passing creates
     a path. My heart unbottles
     all the vintage years.

324 I come a hunter
of secrets. But what is this
beast that stalks my soul?

325 The nation grew up
     on your back. A child rider
     into a cowherd.

326 The heat of noon breaks
     on your brow. Let me be a
     breeze and a shadow.

327   The tree falls in the
forest and no one informs
you. Does the tree fall?

328   All the sea their soup.
The people's servants will have
an emperor's dish.

329   The wind wails into
        every home. We grieve but know
        he won't be the last.

330   Time of the year to
        eat the King. Commoners show
        up, licking their lips.

331 Satan is planning
to sing to us! Take our souls,
if not our money!

332 Let black fire rain
on your heavens! We douse our
rage in Tiger Beer.

333 Yearly, the bodies
     float downstream. Even this will
     be a memory.

334 Not elsewhere but here
     in our differences, the
     same that describes us.

335   The cities war. There
can be no peace until I
find a home in You.

336   In God's City, in
the Houses of God, amid
prayers, the Devil came.

337 Darkness calls. All the
     money in the world can't buy
     you a good night's sleep.

338 Opinions are like
     assholes. Most of us have one.
     Some seem to have lots.

339   Tough times, defiant
      squawks. To silence the chickens,
      we crack a few eggs.

340   Muzzle the dog and
      it swallows its hate. Where do
      barks we don't hear go?

341 A rainbow bends for
the road. I walk on flowers.
Memories of you.

342 All our lives, we have
     been seeing each other. But
     I still need more time.

343 Can't stop now – am on
     a winning streak! Stakes are high,
     but I'm in control!

344 Today in science, we
    see the unseeable. A
    hole looks like a hole.

345 Something must have been
    screenshot because K. woke up
    one morning famous.

346 Facts asks: "Are you an
opinion?" Opinion says:
"Yes, that is a fact."

347 First they warn you. Then
they consult you. Then they make
a law. Then you lose.

348 I think, if you start
     every sentence with "I think",
     you should be OK.

349 My heart takes me out
     for a walk. Freedom is where
     one cannot be found.

350   Darkness remembers
       the light of your faith. The flames
       that kill you restore.

351   Hello, I am a
       celebrity. Come and join
       me for no reason!

352 I watch in silence.
      The wall of words that hides me
      exposes my prey.

353 He's old enough, but
      he's still young. He may be bright,
      but he was stupid.

354 We hear you. We are
     very sorry. Thank you for
     your feedback. Good night.

355 How do you know what
     you don't want to know – if you
     don't know what that is?

356 Memories. A hole
     in my grandfather's roof. The
     monsoon pouring in.

357 At least here we are
     free to die. I pass out from
     your body odour.

358 Not in this dead place —
rather, as freedom among
the living, He lives.

359　"Wolf! Wolf!" cried the boy
　　　in vain. "Beware the boy who
　　　cries wolf," said the wolf.

360　In my Father's house
　　　there is one infrastructure.
　　　Let me prepare it.

361 Democracy is
     under threat! We just don't need
     more people involved.

362 Make sure you succeed
     if you have to kill yourself.
     Or we punish you.

363 A stick is a stick
until it has a ribbon.
Then it's a present.

364 The truth hurts. You are
only as clever as how
dumb your cohort is.

365 I punish me to
    punish you. Then you punish
    me to punish me.

366 The rubber band flies
    further, the more it is stretched.
    It ends when it lands.

367 Water won't break when
    you chop it. Water pipes are
    another matter.

368 Your fire sale burns
    a hole in my pocket. I
    feel both rich and poor.

369 I took someone's seat
     and was given the finger.
     Flipped back a campaign.

370 O cruel lover!
     Now I have lost the backdoor
     into your chamber.

371 From High Olympus
      they come, now daughters of a
      better neighbourhood.

372 To survive, you have
      to eat me. To stop you, I
      have to eat myself.

373   They assured us of
      a green parade. Who among
      us expected tanks?

374   Tanks rumbled to the
      Gates of Peace, over gravestones
      in my memory.

375 Enjoy your dinner!
Sorry I ran over your
mother on the way.

376 The cavalry comes
without its horses. How the
generals waver!

377 Reviled, the college
stands its ground in defiance.
The axed course succeeds.

378 Now your city throws
       petrol bombs. My Gahmen asks:
       "So what have we learnt?"

379 The sun ends its race
       and we begin our own. All
       the world halts for us.

380 "Animals do not
belong in zoos," chimp expert
tells Ah Meng nation.

381 Middle-class, middle-
aged, still haven't found what I'm
looking for. You too?

382 Kids who can't read look
     for Wally. Parents who can't
     read circle swear words.

383 You skip school and you
     lecture us for stealing your
     future? How dare you!

384 When people die, they
      don't come back. It has to be
      this way just because.

385 The House votes are in.
      The orange man turns red and
      yellow like a peach.

386　Chariots of the
　　　gods are racing. Hoofmarks blaze
　　　across my pavement.

387　There will come soft rains
　　　and the smell of embers and
　　　the eagles circling.

388 It's the holidays,
     but the kids are still solving
     maths. My PM too.

389 In a split second,
     are you calm enough to judge?
     Now a schoolboy flies.

390 Happiness ripples
  across his countenance. An
  old man boils his balls.

391 Here is wisdom. Learn
  to laugh at others before
  you laugh at yourself.

392 A poem begins.
You wait for some deep meaning.
Suddenly, it ends.

CONTENTS

ACKNOWLEDGEMENTS

Shared drafts exist for many of these haikus. A few haikus appeared before in the following publications: *Einunddreißig*, 五月诗刊, *SG Poems 2017-2018*, and *Bukit Brown Wayfinder*.

This book's wonderful design and production demonstrate the flair of my publisher Goh Eck Kheng.

ABOUT THE POET

Gwee Li Sui is a Singaporean poet, graphic artist, and literary critic who has published seven other verse collections: *Who Wants to Buy a Book of Poems?* (1998), *One Thousand and One Nights* (2014), *Who Wants to Buy an Expanded Edition of a Book of Poems?* (2015), *The Other Merlion and Friends* (2015), *Haikuku* (2017), and *Death Wish* (2017).

A familiar name in Singapore's cultural scene, Gwee has been writing and lecturing on a wide range of subjects, from English literature to Singlish.

He has edited numerous acclaimed anthologies, including *Written Country: The History of Singapore through Literature* (2016).